No tinkering with postures that gambit faceless coins across the waiting well
Only humming with certain soothing breaths that leave the heart embossed with velvet
Only strumming the threads that bind your closeness to its picturesque summit
Which don't interrogate the nerves of needless crumbling pixelated aftermath
The droves of chorused engineers that light your starlit canvas
Speak only of your wishful authenticity most gracefully and graciously
They are the loveliest lettering that gleams upon the unbroken braids of your destiny
Don't entrench yourself in the wistful webbed strain of your own clutching breathlessness
But unbow its knees and make love to the stillness that waits no more
And there upon the shores of your last gasping grievances
Are you unburdened by mortality and enlivened with endless depth of soulful selfhood
To begin is to already have begun, and to end is never enough
But with sleep of stagnant disheartening worship
And the glow of footsteps whose burgeoning courageous acumen accept
That a drop of sand in the silvery notions of your purchasing one more moment of
daylight in creation
And the treating of its honest boldness easily touches you with one calming careful
gladness wrapped with love of light
The way and sun that has set will shine higher and brighter than any racing currents
And summon the whole of you with great symphony and certain triumph
To a place that was once and was always growing more lovely
And a face that is yours to behold and adore for all timeless

✳

REALITY IS OPTIONAL

Mood Work, Magic, and Mastery

from the Vortex Edge

Jeff Utter

A mythic invitation disguised as a book

Self-published in the United States
First Edition

Cover design, interior layout, and alignment magic by Jeff Utter
Made with joy, channeling, and starlight.

For Stacy.

*And for anyone who's ever stopped efforting long
enough to float.*

CONTENTS

Introduction: Reality Called—You Don't Have to Answer 1

Chapter One: Mood Is the Remote 13

Chapter Two: The Vortex Already Sent the Invite 31

Chapter Three: Dreamer's License Activated 45

Chapter Four: How to Stop Spiraling About Spiraling 63

Chapter Five: Pull This Lever and Watch Reality Blush 83

Chapter Six: Let It Land Like You're Not Micromanaging a Miracle 99

ॐ

Bonus: The Mood Ladder 109

Outro: You Are the Dream and the Dumb Genius Who Forgot 121

INTRODUCTION

Reality Called—You Don't Have to Answer (Unless It's Delivering Synchronicity and Snacks)

A Slightly Inappropriate Guide to Greatness

Welcome to the edge of the unseen—a place of miracles with a side of mischief, invisible nudges, and the dream that's halfway through writing your name in stardust.

This book is the result of a lifetime lived with eyes and heart wide open. I've wandered, created, loved, fallen, risen, lost and found myself, and danced with more than a few paradoxes along the way. Through it all, I've come to understand some things that feel profoundly true—truths I lived into, and ones that came into focus through teachings like Abraham-Hicks, which I've danced with for nearly twenty years.

It also came from a single conversation—one Sunday morning—with a group of like-minded co-authors of reality. We met inside a sacred container I once imagined—then watched materialize like some sort of mystical group chat made real. That space became a kind of portal. And from within it, something landed.

1

What emerged was this book.

Part activation. Part cosmic permission slip. Part mirror that winks when you look too closely.

It's also a collection of irreverent little portals disguised as questions—designed not just to make you laugh, but to gently jailbreak your programming while making you laugh-snort, and to offer you a broader, lighter, more playful perspective on yourself, your life, and your role in this ridiculous masterpiece we call reality.

These questions weren't strategized—they arrived like lightning bugs—unexpected and full of glow. Some came while walking. Some while laughing. Some while lying on the floor wondering why none of the "manifestation techniques" were working—until I remembered that feeling good *was* the manifestation.

The questions aren't the point. The feeling they unlock is. And if you're the type who finds that feeling through a long hot shower, a playlist that makes your heart sing, a walk in your favorite shoes, or a single perfectly timed meme—that's perfectly wonderful! That's alignment. That's you, in the pocket.

It's all wonderful, because anything that feels good to you is your higher self saying, "Yes—this is the way. We're right here with you." It doesn't matter what subject or process you use to get into alignment, it only matters how it feels. If it feels good to you, it is good for you.

Still, I thought I'd share these questions with you—not as a

method, but more like spiritual mischief with benefits. They've worked wonders for me. Here are some examples of what I might ask myself instead of trying to brute-force the cosmos with my forehead:

◆ "If the Universe had a 'Treat Yourself' button, would I press it—or workshop my way out of it until the portal ghosts me?"

◆ "Am I feeling my frequency—or just catastrophizing in high-resolution?"

◆ "What if the thing I'm trying to manifest is already knocking and I keep yelling, 'Hang on, I'm scripting!'?"

◆ "Right now, would my Inner Being be laughing, applauding, or quietly texting me 'Please make the next available U-turn.'?"

◆ "If this moment were a movie, would I still be stuck in the training montage—or am I lowkey already in the champagne-and-confetti-afterparty and forgot to RSVP myself?"

Questions like these showed up when I stopped trying to be right and started playing with the frequency. They didn't fix anything. They unclenched the vibe. They left the door cracked for resonance to sneak in wearing something fabulous.

This book is a collection of those moments—distilled. It's a field of reminders, reflections, invitations. Not to escape life, but to feel into it more vividly. More freely. More specifically, when it feels good to do so. More generally, when it doesn't.

So yeah. That's the vibe check.

You don't have to hustle your way to worthiness. You don't have to believe in your dream fully before you're allowed to enjoy today. You don't even have to answer the call of 'reality' unless it's holding snacks and winking.

You are not here to fix yourself. You're here to remember the signal you came with.

Your mood is the remote.

Your joy is the password.

And your vibe is the only algorithm that matters.

This book won't walk you through a three-step technique with clenched jaw and spreadsheets. It's more of a vibe-lifter. A sacred permission slip wrapped in humor. A loose transmission from your higher self disguised as a slightly inappropriate beach read.

Let it land softly.

And if you're ready to let go, crack up, tune in, and start living like your Inner Being is the star of a divine improv show...

Then fasten your seatbelt and unfasten your seriousness.

Let this be a mirror. A frequency. A remembering. Welcome to the liminal lounge of your favorite frequency—where blessings loiter and breakthroughs flirt. The vibe is delicious. The answers are funny. And the dream? It's already dreaming you back.

Your mood is the remote. Your joy is the password. And your vibe is the algorithm the universe actually checks.

CHAPTER ONE

Mood Is the Remote (And You've Been Watching the Wrong Channel)

So here's what I realized: you're not obligated to face any version of reality that dims your glow. Truly. You're not required to rent space in your attention to anything that taxes your light. Because focus is fuel—and whatever you feed with attention starts broadcasting louder. You're keeping it going.

And I get it. Reality can be persuasive. It's vivid. It yells in 3D. Sometimes with unpaid bills and extra attitude. But still... it's just a habit of focus. That's all.

Everything you see around you started in imagination. Everything. Even this moment. Even the "facts" you think you're dealing with. They became solid because you gave them your attention—and attention creates gravity. So if it's not lighting you up, change the channel.

Mood is the remote. It's the only setting we truly have control over.

Not your circumstances. Not other people. Not the plot twists in your inbox. Just your mood. And once you get that—really

get it—you stop trying to reorganize the world so you can feel better. You flip the order: feel better, then watch the hologram reshuffle itself like it got the memo.

You stop trying to wrestle reality into submission with spiritual elbow grease. You align—and let your reality fall into place.

☙

Sometimes, when I need a gentle shift, I ask myself a question that wakes up my spirit. Something playful. Something unexpectedly true. Then I answer it, not to fix anything—but to feel like my favorite version of me again. Like:

"What's the easiest way to be me on purpose right now?"

⟹ *Say the outrageous thing. Do the thing that makes no sense but feels right. Then ride that wild wave until your future self gives you a high five and a forehead kiss through space-time.*

And suddenly I'm grinning like the air told a joke only I could hear. I feel the static clear. I feel my cells remember their passwords. I forget to pretend I'm normal and start glowing on accident like a firefly with excellent Wi-Fi.

Here's another fun one:

"If joy were currency, how rich would I be in the next 10 minutes?"

⟹ Filthy. Stupid-rich. Like "build a yacht shaped like a cinnamon roll" rich. You just have to stop refreshing your emotional Venmo like a desperate manifestor with no chill.

That one hits like champagne in a dream. Like, of course I'm ridiculous with riches — they just happen to be vibrational. I stop budgeting joy like it's on rations and start spending like joy's got rollover minutes.

"What part of me is already winning so hard it's embarrassing the rest of me?"

⟹ The Inner Being part lounging in velvet robes, sipping light-infused lattes, whispering sweet truths to the rest of me that's still refreshing the worry feed.

I laugh out loud. My resistance can't even pretend to be in charge anymore. I picture my Inner Being in a 5D spa made of stardust and giggles, chuckling gently as I spiral. And in that moment, I spiral back up.

These kinds of questions—what I call vibration activators—remind

me that alignment isn't a chore. It's recess for your soul. And I get to play.

It's wild how much relief comes when you stop resisting your resistance. I used to double down on myself the moment I dipped below joy, like I owed the universe an apology. Like, "You know better than this! You teach this stuff!" But that just made it worse. That's not mastery. That's judgment.

Real mastery is soft. It's velvety. It's sweet.

It's letting yourself off the hook while mid-wobble, mid-flop, mid-oh-god-not-again and saying, "Hey. It's okay. You're allowed to be human today."

And here's the part that surprised me: even imagining something just a little better than what's in front of you is enough. You don't have to go all the way to bliss. You just have to look in the direction of what you want. That's it. That's the whole game. You want to know how to move up the emotional scale? Just ask yourself: What would the next-better feeling actually feel like in my body right now?

So sometimes I pretend. I don't mean pretend like fake it—I mean imagine.

I give myself permission to take what I call...

Imaginative License.

If I'm in a dungeon—emotional, financial, metaphorical, planetary, take your pick—I either look for the gold bricks in that dungeon, or I close my eyes and I imagine myself on a beach. With someone I love. In a moment that feels like freedom. And when I do that, something real happens. The walls don't just disappear metaphorically. They literally shift. Reality has to change. It has no choice.

The less I grip reality, the happier I get. The more I play with possibility, the more real those possibilities become. The less I try to wrangle reality, the more it sweetens. The more I lean into joy, the more joy leans back. And that's not delusion. That's how the mechanism works. That's creation. You wouldn't accuse a seed of being delusional just because it hasn't sprouted leaves.

Then something even deeper begins to unfold...

It shows me that I'm not just a participant in this life—I'm the radiant architect of it. Not to prove my worth—but to feel it. It shows me that I am a magnificent, marvelous masterpiece. It shows me that I have depth beyond description. That I am anointed—constructed from, made of—pure loving light. It shows me that I only care about love, passion, exhilaration, deep peace, and joy. That only in those places am I truly dealing with anything that matters. It shows me unequivocally that I do not care about one single thing that doesn't ring my bells. I remember that I care only about what makes me come alive. That everything

else is background noise.

In fact, it even shows me that I love those things I don't care about too—because I am one who only loves, who only trusts, who only succeeds, no matter how convincing the surface gets with its storyline in a moment. It shows me that I understand the value of all experience: the benefit it provides, the texture it creates, the space it carves out for the beauty and joy of life and love. And so I am absolutely, utterly unperturbed by any of it. In fact, I adore it. I appreciate it.

It shows me that I see no lack, no shortage, no problem, no disparity, no incongruity anywhere. Turns out, incongruity is just congruity in a costume.

It shows me that I cannot escape my fate as a brilliant, beaming beacon of faithfulness and trust in the all-pervading well-being of my Self, my story, and my spark.

It shows me that what's behind me is loveliness unending. That what's before me is imperfect perfection dancing with exquisiteness. That what's ahead of me is an aurora. A frontier. A torrential avalanche of brilliance, blessings, and bliss. That there is not one single thing I need to do, or ever needed to do—but that I stand in boundless, everlasting opportunity wrapped in immutable glory and drenched in fantastically blessed good fortune of self, world, and universe.

So that's where I start. That's where I always start: Mood first. Mood is the gateway. The brush. The spell. And honestly? Feeling good is enough.

I can't count the times I've seen myself and others on this path asking the fervent question, "Is feeling good enough? Does it really work? Can I just feel good and what I want will flow?" We so want it to be true and ask in burning desperation whether we can truly release our white-knuckle grip on control and let the stream carry us straight to everything our joy's been magnetizing all along..

And I want to shout outwardly, inwardly, to myself, and to all those who are asking with everything they are: "Yes! Yes! Yes! That's it. That's the whole spell. That's the move."

Try it. Let yourself go there—and just *watch* what unfolds. Don't wait for results before you let yourself *know* that feeling good is enough—just try it earnestly, fully, unequivocally.

Feeling good is enough. That's not the consolation prize—that's the main event. And everything else flows from there. I promise you.

&

*Feeling good is enough. It's every-
thing. It's not the side dish. It's the
spell. And everything else flows from
there.*

CHAPTER TWO

The Universe Already Sent the Invite—You Just Keep Checking Spam

I didn't have to fix anything. That was the wild, revolutionary, almost suspiciously simple realization. Like it had no business working so well. It didn't arrive all at once—but in pulses. Sparks. Like the universe kept blinking from behind the static. A little spark-flare saying, "Hey, it's already here."

The part of me still trying to body-slam contrast into clarity? Fried. But the part that paused—listened, softened, stopped trying to "figure it out"? That part was onto something. That part was already aligned.

I started to imagine that the version of reality I wanted was already assembled. Not someday. Not if I earned it. But now. Already assembled. Just waiting for me to notice. My job wasn't to force it into place—it was just to align with it. To tune in like it was already broadcasting.

I started asking, "What does the high-vibration version of this look like?" "What does the version of this feel like that's already humming with alignment?" Not to control what's "real"—but to remember that what's real is flexible.

It's not fixed. It's a channel. And I'm the dial.

"Am I rowing the boat or riding the dolphin? (And if it's a jet ski, why am I paddling?)"

⟹ *You've already built a joy-powered reality, and here you are gripping a plastic oar like your life depends on it.*

I was efforting in places where I was meant to float. All I had to do was trust the current already carrying me.

The less I faced reality, the better my reality got. Not in a bypass-y, la-la land way. But in a deeply intentional way. The less I tried to fix reality, the better it got—not in a denial kind of way, but in a responsibility upgrade kind of way. Because every time I obsessed over the problem, I was just re-magnetizing it. Every time I argued for the limitation, I was keeping it alive. So I stopped trying to fix the dungeon. And I started imagining the beach. And wouldn't you know—it didn't take long before a window appeared in the wall. Then a breeze. Then the whole thing melted away like a rerun I finally stopped watching.

That's what this work is. Not fixing the dream. Not arguing with it. But dreaming better. Feeling better. Being better—not in behavior, but in broadcast.

The broadcast is everything.

33

Sometimes, when I'm fuzzy or fried, I ask myself:

"What's the 'hell yes' under this 'meh maybe'?"

⟹ There's a rocket of desire lodged under your maybe—it just got wrapped in caution tape. Peel back the safety protocol and listen for the part that makes your whole body grin.

Because there's always a signal under the static. A song under the noise. A click, a thrum, a glimmer—proof that yes, even this part is divine.

Sometimes I think back on the times reality was trying to send a message, and I just wildly misinterpreted the vibe—like a charades rookie shouting 'BOAT! WRENCH! SELF-SABOTAGE!' at full volume, while the Vortex was clearly miming "You're doing amazing, sweetie—please go nap."

I remember not feeling well enough to go to work and spinning out about it. Instead of seeing it as the lovingly-timed get-out-of-resistance-free card it was, I spiraled into "This is my fault," or "I should have done better," or "Maybe I need to get better at adulting and eating more broccoli." Even my dearest beliefs—about alignment, magic, flow—would get tossed like expired milk.

But what it was actually saying was: "*We didn't see you all that excited about what you were doing anyway!* You look like you're

35

trying to run a marathon with your shoes tied together blindfolded—when you're actually due to be sipping mimosas with your favorite characters at the celebration of It-Was-Never-A-Race-And-You've-Already-Won-Palooza."

ঌ

That's when I realized: The part of me that's not physical—the energetic self, the bigger me—has been nudging me all along.

It wasn't that I missed the signs. I just misread them. Mistook 'rest' for 'ruin,' and 'pause' for 'problem.' Mistook 'detour' for 'dead end.' Now, if the vibes feel off, I don't assume I'm broken. I assume I've got mail.

I don't have to face anything I don't want to live. I don't have to attend to anything just because others are obsessing over it. I don't have to look at anything unless it delights me to do so. I don't stare at what drags me down just because it's on the screen. I remember:

Reality is not a brick wall. It's a mirror. And the moment I stop arguing with the reflection and start reaching for a better inner landscape—reality starts catching up to me.

And it always does. Always-always.

Still, sometimes I catch myself making a really convincing case for my limitations. Like I'm laying out internal evidence for why I don't 'get' to feel good... yet.

Maybe it's, "I know I'm supposed to trust the process, but look at all this stuff I still haven't figured out."

Suddenly I'm building a whole thesis on misalignment—calling it realism, and pretending I'm excited about the topic. It would be better to ask myself something like:

> ## "Am I manifesting the life I want to live, or just aggressively narrating my own resistance in a fun font?"
>
> *⇒ Spoiler: You've been using Comic Sans to rationalize your vibe dip. Time to switch to Bold Italic Trust and let the plot breathe.*

That's a powerful shift! Because when I remember that my job isn't to fix the outer world—it's just to stop paddling upstream—everything shifts. The static clears. The dolphin does a backflip. And I'm back.

That's the thing I keep forgetting, and remembering again: The dream doesn't need fixing. The signal's already broadcasting. My only job is to tune in. And when I do—I remember: I was never disconnected. I was just checking the wrong inbox.

The dolphin does a backflip. And I'm back.

CHAPTER THREE

Dreamer's License Activated—Use Imagination Responsibly (Or Don't)

What if imagining it wasn't the prelude—what if it was the entire spell?

I used to treat imagination like a preview. But it's not the preview. It's not the blueprint—it's the painting. Not the rehearsal—it's opening night.

Imagination isn't the warmup for life. It is life—written from the inside out. And the moment I stop asking "Is this real?" and start asking "Do I love this scene?"—everything begins to rearrange.

You're allowed to stop tuning to what doesn't fit. You stop rehearsing realities you don't even want. You stop reanimating scenes just because they showed up before.

That's the whole cheat code. Don't gaslight yourself into love— just remember: if it doesn't feel like the full you, it's not the whole truth. It's not the highest-frequency track. And if it's not that track, why stay in it? Why not dip into the scene that already clicks?

The one that tunes your cells like the bass just dropped on your actual life....

When the vision lights up your insides. When the daydream that keeps tapping on your shoulder finally gets your attention.

That's where I feel the click. Not the checklist kind. Not the productivity kind. But that soul-click. The "ohhh yeahhh" click. The one that feels like slipping into your realest skin.

"Can I feel the click of a soul yes... or am I trying to get inspiration to do pushups in a mud puddle of obligation?"

⇒ You already know. If it feels like obligation Pilates, it's not it. If it feels like, "Oh sh*t, I get to do this??" That's the click.

That click is the compass now. I don't chase what doesn't light me up. I don't analyze what drains me just because it showed up on today's screen. Because I know that life is akin to a dream.

We've all had weird dreams. Some are even awful, some maybe just uncomfortable. But you don't wake up and obsess over them for three days... unless you want them back. Same goes for life.

It's all dream-coded anyway—thought-responsive, mood-shaped, storyline-sensitive.

So I've learned not to linger in versions of reality that don't match who I'm becoming. If it doesn't meet me with clarity, joy, or resonance—I trust that it's not the one to answer right now.

You gotta let go of what isn't ringing your bells. Or see it in a new light that does. That's the magic. That's the art. That's the license. Take it. Use your writer's license. Your dreamer's license. Your infinite re-authoring ability.

> "What would I create if I stopped caring how it would perform and started caring how it would feel?"

⟹ *You'd make something so electrifying it would giggle your atoms loose. A creation so full of YOU it would smell like a thunderstorm and taste like freedom.*

Because this whole "life" setup? It bends for imagination. Not the other way around.

It took me a while to fully believe that. Not because I didn't want to, but because I kept checking on things. You know? "Is it working yet?" And every time I checked, I'd slip back into the old channel. I was measuring a miracle with a yardstick I got from Walmart's clearance bin. I was shooting my own belief

in the foot with yesterday's metric. Which is like making a wish and immediately yelling, "Are we there yet?!"

But then something clicks in a moment. A moment of relaxing. I let go, even just for a second, of the need to micromanage the entire unfolding. And I feel it: that unmistakable hum of "ohhh... it's already done."

And then it becomes obvious—every time I imagine what I want, I am creating it. Right now. Right here. Not someday. Not later. Now. The act of imagining it is the act of birthing it into this version of the dream. And every time I imagine what I *don't* want, I'm creating that too.

"If imagination creates reality, who cast this scene?"

⟹ *Oh right. You did. Mid-scroll. While dehydrated. It's okay—you can recast now.*

That's why I always say: don't get stuck facing reality like it's some non-negotiable, static Earth script. That would be like watching a weird dream and going, "Welp, guess this is what I'm stuck with tonight."

Nah. No thanks. I choose lucidity.

☙

So now, if I don't like what I'm seeing, I close my eyes and see

something else. Or I open them wider and see the hidden shimmer in what's already there. Either way, I'm wielding my dreamer's license. Not in denial—but in authorship.

And in that authorship, I've realized... every moment is a brushstroke. A cue. A plot point. Every mood is a line of dialogue in the story I'm telling myself. So if I want a better story, I don't need to fight the plot—just shift the genre.

> ## "What creation would future-me look back on and say 'Dude, that's the one'?"

> ⟹ *The one you made when you were laughing. When you weren't trying to prove anything. The thing that felt like skipping instead of striving. That one.*

Sometimes I daydream something so outrageously unrealistic... it starts to feel suspiciously inevitable.

Like I see Future Me looking wildly radiant, like "whoa, have you been drinking sunlight and doing affirmations with dolphins?" Hair's glossier. Eyes are glinting with secret victories. There's a vibe like I just got back from a retreat on another planet—and I was the guest speaker. Even the way I walk says, "Yeah, the timeline upgraded. Try to keep up."

There's money in my pockets, in my drawers, in the glovebox, careening through my bank account—like it naturally wants to

be near me and flow through me. And I'm strolling through luxury like it's a Tuesday. The abundance flows with grace, ease, and perfect timing. And the Universe just keeps delivering.

In that version of the dream, I'm building joy-first empires. Making art that slaps souls awake. Writing books like it's breathwork. Dancing in music videos I score myself. Dropping truth-bombs like TikToks for mystics.

I'm taking my girl to places we used to call dreams—rooftops, oceans, ancient forests lit with laughter. We speak fluent stardust and make memories so beautiful they hum. We vanish into private wonderlands. We kiss like we invented it. We rest. We play. We disappear when we want to. We fall more in love every day.

Me and my son are laughing in matching jackets at a vintage arcade. Beating high scores, talking smack, making memories out of pixels and pizza slices.

Later, we're back on the land—our land. The treehouses I built for us are strung across the trees like an Ewok village, with rope bridges and hammocks and solar lights that glow like fireflies at night. We live up there when we feel like it.

My mom sipping tea somewhere soft, looking peaceful in a way I always wished for her, while she laughs watching the young kids playing.

We spend the afternoon with her while she shows us the paintings she's been making—abstract skies, vibrant fields, faces that feel

like memories. She's glowing, proud in the quiet way that says, "I finally gave myself permission to enjoy this." The light catches the edges of her canvas and her joy fills the whole room.

All of us around a firepit—my brother, his fam, the whole crew—telling stories that only get funnier with time.

Then it cuts to winter: I've whisked everyone off to a dream-lodge in the mountains for Christmas. A roaring fire, snow falling slow, music echoing through wooden beams. And under the tree? So many gifts, we needed a second one.

Everyone laughing, unwrapping, stunned. I'm just watching it all unfold, heart wide open, because I could.

And the wildest part? All of this feels truer than half the stuff people call "real." It feels like a leaked spoiler from my own autobiography. And I've decided—I'm not waiting to see if it happens. I'm just gonna live it from the inside out.

From dystopia to magical realism. From burden to blessing. From dungeon to dancefloor.

Because whether I'm in the middle of some life situation that feels immovable—or just vibing gently through a regular day—there is always a more thrilling lens available. There is always a version I can tune into on a better channel. And I have access. Right now. Every time. I'm the one with the pen.

ॐ

From dungeon to dancefloor.

HEART   SPARK   UAK

CHAPTER FOUR

How to Stop Spiraling About Spiraling (a.k.a. Loving Your Mess Is Hot)

One thing keeps surprising me, over and over: the mess is never the problem. The judgment of it is.

Instead it's about no longer being upset at myself for being upset. No longer resisting my resistance. No longer spiraling because I'm spiraling. That's the thing that has made the biggest difference. When that layer drops, softness enters. The storm quiets. A gentleness takes over. I stop trying to strong-arm myself back into a better mood. I stop trying to fix it all. I stop trying to not be where I am.

It turns out the key isn't to avoid resistance entirely—it's to stop resisting that I have resistance. That's the doorway into emotional mastery. The moment I stop adding more pressure to the pressure, I soften. I allow. I don't push the river.

I don't make myself wrong for not being in a higher vibration. I don't make myself feel bad about feeling bad. I let myself be. I let the moment be. I stop spiraling about spiraling, and somehow... I begin to float.

"How do you know you're softening into alignment?"

⟹ *When even your spiral has snacks and ambient lighting.*

There's a kind of softness that becomes strength. There's a kind of allowing that becomes alignment. There's a kind of wobble that becomes wisdom.

What used to feel like emotional regression starts to feel like evolution. Not a step backward—just a fuller view of the whole picture. Not a failure to stay in alignment—just a deeper invitation to trust even more. Not the death of progress—just the expansion of compassion.

When I experience this, I notice that I stop judging the clouds for not being the sun. I start listening instead. I let the emotion pass through without labeling it wrong. I let the sadness be sacred. I let the frustration be fuel. I let the doubt be interesting. I stop making every feeling into a scorecard on how well I'm doing. Emotion becomes guidance instead of a verdict.

There's no pop quiz. There's no perfect track record. There's no gold star for staying happy all day. There's just the signal. And the signal is here to help. This is where you realize:

"Oh, that feeling I've been calling wrong? That's actually my guidance system working perfectly."

65

We were never meant to hate the signal. But we were taught to. Somewhere along the way, we mistook guidance for punishment and emotion for misbehavior. As if feeling off meant something was broken in us—when really, it was just the dashboard light saying, "Hey love, different road."

And the moment you stop being mad at the indicator? You're free. Because not panicking about negative emotion is emotional mastery. It's when you stop screaming at the thermometer and start tending to the fire. It's when your reaction to the wobble becomes love instead of judgment.

That's the turn. That's the unlock.

> ## "Is this a lesson, or is this me refusing to vibe higher until I finish my imaginary punishment sandwich?"

> ⟹ *You're 87% through the sandwich. Toss the rest and go get dessert. There is no pop quiz. Just vibes.*

Real growth doesn't ask for essays and diagrams. It doesn't want you to over-explain your trauma one more time before you're allowed to feel good. It just wants you to stop arguing with the mirror long enough to dance with your reflection.

Sometimes the most spiritually aligned thing you can do is abandon the "shoulds," laugh mid-sentence, and eat the damn

dessert.

I said it during a recent Sunday session in our Law of Attraction Mastermind, and I meant it with my whole being:

When you remove your resistance to your resistance, you've pretty much removed the resistance.

Boom.

It was true with emotional pain. It was true with physical pain. It was true with confusion, sadness, jealousy, overwhelm. It was always the resistance to the emotion that hurt the most—not the emotion itself. Once I let the energy have its way with me... I begin to float.

And sometimes, I float in ways that would make a motivational speaker sweat through their tucked-in polo. Like, I've literally said to my fears and doubts, "Hey team, I see you. Let's take the weekend off. You don't have to leave, but you do have to shut up. We'll reconvene Monday and get back to second-guessing everything my heart knows is true then, cool?"

Oddly, they accept it.

And then I just vibe. Like really vibe. Lay around all damn day if it feels good. Do only what I actually 100% feel like doing. No pushing. No guilt trips. Just straight-up emotional vacation. And wouldn't you know—Monday rolls around and boom: extension granted. Money arrives. Plans shift. A gentle reschedule

nudge from the Universe that says, "Let's keep the good vibes rolling a little longer, yeah?"

This has happened not once, but many times. Like... weeks and months of flow unfolding because I dared to be radically lazy in a way that looked illegal to my former self. And some of the most important things in my life came from that space— new business, healthier love, deeper peace.

❧

It's not about performing the perfect vibrational routine. It's about relaxing the grip. Sometimes it means laying on the floor. Sometimes it means dancing. Sometimes it means eating the cookies and not giving a single damn. Sometimes it means turning off the affirmations and watching something dumb until your nervous system forgets what it was freaking out about.

When that permission shows up, everything starts to breathe. Real growth doesn't require emotional perfection. Real growth includes weirdness. Real growth includes spirals. Real growth includes "I thought I was past this" moments. Real growth includes you, exactly as you are.

Sometimes contrast is just contrast. Sometimes resistance is just weather. Sometimes being down doesn't mean you're doing it wrong. Sometimes it just means you're in the middle of the good part.

"What's the joke I'm missing that would make this whole thing funny instead of frustrating?"

⟹ That you keep yelling 'Where's the door?!' in a room made of curtains. You're not trapped. You're just being dramatic. And it's hilarious.

The spiral isn't personal. It's not trying to take you down. It's not evidence of failure. It's not proof that you've lost your touch. It's not the universe ghosting you.

It's just a moment. And it's okay to stop pushing. It's okay to sit down. It's okay to float.

That's the paradox. That's the step that doesn't feel like a step. That's the spiral cracking open into softness. That's the shift that doesn't scream. That's the mastery that isn't measured.

Not everything needs to be processed. Not everything needs to be journaled. Not everything needs to be transmuted. Sometimes it just needs to be not resisted.

That's our power. That's real leverage. That's the secret-sauce velvetness of not spiraling about spiraling. And I'll tell you something wild: that softness? That surrender? That's when I start to feel powerful. Not when I force my way into clarity. Not when I demand alignment. But when I lean back into it. When I allow the stream to carry me without thrashing against

the current. That's the truest kind of strength I've ever known.

"What would it look like to be completely safe while feeling this?"

⇒ Like sipping celestial tea in a gravity-free cuddle cloud while existence plays you a lo-fi playlist made of compliments and angels fan you with acceptance.

That's high-level. It's emotional self-trust. It's vibrational forgiveness. It's choosing not to spiral about spiraling. It's feeling the wobble and not building a whole identity around it. It's noticing the contrast and not writing a twelve-paragraph story about what it must mean.

It's letting the wobble be temporary, because it is. And suddenly, the wobble is welcome.

The doubt is no longer devouring everything. The shame loses its megaphone. The mind stops screaming. And the heart gets to whisper. The moment becomes livable again. Then sweet again. Then powerful again.

"What if the Universe is watching me like a sitcom right now and waiting for the big breakthrough laugh?"

⟹ You're mid-slapstick, slipping on the
banana peel of doubt. Cue the laugh track.
Don't worry—the big reveal scene is next.
It involves glitter and unexpected backpay.

It's funny because it's real. Because sometimes your breakthrough starts in the middle of a breakdown where you're muttering to yourself while staring at the ceiling fan like it owes you rent.

And that's okay. The universe doesn't need you to be poised. It just needs you to stay in the scene long enough to catch the punchline.

Because the moment you stop resisting the absurdity of your own arc? You realize the mess was just the moment the magic got bored of hiding. Invite the mess in for lunch, and remind it to come back again any time it's in the neighborhood.

❧

"If I were the final boss
of my own limitations,
what move would I not see
coming?"

⟹ *Radical joy. Just straight-
up choosing to feel awesome
for no reason. That'd break
the game's code and crash
your resistance in a shower of
sparkles.*

CHAPTER FIVE

Pull This Lever and Watch Reality Blush

Mood First. Magic Follows.

You can let go of the ten thousand levers. The strategies. The overthinking. The backup plans for the backup plans.

There's only one lever that actually does anything.

Mood.

That's the lever. And it controls everything else. Every result you're chasing. Every client. Every opportunity. Every dollar. Every encounter. Every synchronicity. Every miracle.

That one lever cues it all.

And the moment the grip on effort softens—even slightly— everything gets lighter. Like life finally exhales and says, "Thanks, we've been waiting for you."

We don't realize how hard we've been trying until we stop. Until we let ourselves stop. We keep thinking we need to be productive. Strategic. Intentional. But when we get quiet, when we drop all the weighty effort and just focused on feeling

good—everything else gets lighter too.

And life starts moving. Not because we're pushing it forward, but because we finally let the current carry us.

ॐ

"How do you pull the lever that makes reality blush?"

⟹ Sing off-key. Wink at the mirror. Declare yourself hot and unstoppable while making toast.

So the shift happens. You stop trying to fix the vibe like it's a group project and you're the only one doing the work. You stop micro-managing your manifestations like the universe is your underperforming intern. You stop clenching your soul like it owes you results.

And in that delicious absence of effort, something sneaky happens: The mood lifts. The music gets louder. The air feels flirtier. You catch yourself smiling at nothing. You accidentally align.

Not because you "did the work," but because you stopped treating your life like a spreadsheet and started treating it like a vibe.

A better mood. A breath. A laugh. A goosebump song. A better-feeling thought. That's the magic wand.

And reality... responds.

That's when reality blushes. And then... it gets generous.

Sometimes the thing that flips everything for me isn't "doing the work" at all. It's booty-shaking to a song that isn't even playing. It's narrating what strangers are doing on the sidewalk like I'm hosting a wildlife documentary for my son. It's singing a deliberately bad 80s ballad that never should've existed—featuring the name of someone I love and a chorus no one asked for.

I've serenaded my girlfriend with "Good Morning and I Wuv You So Much" hundreds of times, off the chart-smashing mixtape Weird Stuff My Brain Comes Up With. (It kinda slaps. Don't ask.)

I've pummeled my son's consciousness with my other classic, "Das My Guy, Das Mah' Dude," for no other reason than I believe in annoyingly repetitive affection as a love language.

And sometimes I just yell straight-up gibberish to the ceiling in the morning like it's a pregame stretch.

"SHMIMSHBIMSH SHCOBBY WOBBY!!"

And the multiverse, I swear to Source, is like: "If you say so, King. Cue the sunshine and hummingbirds—he's on the move."

That's the lever. Right there. Not a spreadsheet. Not a breakthrough. Just play. Just presence. Just a moment where joy snuck in and rewrote the script.

And the beautiful thing? When joy leads, everything else tends to follow. Not just mood. Not just energy. Actual things. Unexpected upgrades. Glorious human plot twists.

Your body feels better, your relationships improve, the situations that play out in your life are more in harmony with what you are wanting. Your money flows more easily. (I'm guessing at least one or two people reading this wouldn't mind more money.)

Not because you chanted into a crystal while standing on your tax returns, but because joy messes with the laws of probability like it's on a sugar high.

When you're vibing right, money gets curious. It peeks in the window like, "Y'all having fun in here?"

And you're like, "Yeah, but bring snacks."

And it does.

"What if money wasn't the reward for work but the confetti for alignment?"

⇒ *Then you'd stop scanning your to-do list and start scanning your joy meter. When it hits "tingly smirk," the money hits "incoming transfer."*

Life always responds to the lever you're actually pulling.

So now I don't ask, "What should I do?" I ask, "What would feel better right now?"

And that question? It's the master key. Every time.

And when I let myself answer it without guilt, without second-guessing, without trying to make it "practical"—I get the weirdest results. Fast. Easy. Magical. Because when the vibe is right, reality gets giddy. Things start flowing. Clients, checks, miracles in your inbox.

But you gotta get the feeling before you can see any of these manifestations. It's about making the feeling be the manifestation you're reaching for. Figure out how you would feel if the things you want were already true and then don that attitude now!

> ## "If I already had way more money than I knew what to do with, what dumb fun thing would I do next?"

> ⟹ *You'd buy your girl a rainbow-shaped hot tub, order a diamond-encrusted journal labeled "Silly Sh*t That Works," and fund a psychedelic sock line that somehow saves bees.*

Sometimes the answer is so delicious, it makes you blush. Sometimes the answer is so weird, it makes you laugh. And the Vortex is already nodding like, "You want that in lavender or teal?"

That's the magic of asking the right question — it doesn't pull in logic. It pulls in a frequency. And the answers that come back? They're already tuned to yes.

It also means releasing the constant need to know exactly how the things you think you want are going to manifest. You don't need to know how it's gonna happen! You just need to know how you want to feel—and tune yourself into that feeling by any means necessary. Even if that means using your imagination. (I know some of us hung up our imaginations when we were kids and grew up too fast.) Or even if it means being a little silly—or, god forbid, having fun.

"Am I tuned to the frequency of 'yes,' or still scrolling the AM static of 'how'?"

⟹ *You're toggling. But every time you laugh, say "f*ck it," or dance in the kitchen, you jump back to 'yes.' Keep flipping to that station. It plays your theme song.*

This is the whole jam.

Mood is the portal. Joy is the password. Ease is the access point.

Every time you feel good for no reason, the world reshapes itself around you. Because the lever you're pulling is the only one that ever mattered.

"Where am I still negotiating with scarcity like it's my landlord instead of a confused raccoon in my psychic attic?"

⟹ *That voice that says "be responsible" while clutching a coupon book and whispering guilt? Yeah, that's the raccoon. It doesn't pay rent. Show it the door.*

CHAPTER SIX

Let It Land Like You're Not Micromanaging a Miracle

You don't need to remember everything you just read. You don't need to memorize steps, highlight sections, or do anything at all with this book... unless you want to.

Because the real shift doesn't happen in the thinking. It happens in the tuning. The click. The soft yes. The moment something inside you whispered, "Ohhh... that."

"How do you know you've tuned into alignment?"

⇛ *You start smiling at spoons, dancing at red lights, and calling your future self 'babe.'*

That's the frequency we're relaxing into.

This isn't a manual. It's a mirror. And if you saw even a glint of your true self in these pages, that's the work complete. The rest is just resonance.

You're already practicing it. Every time you reach for the slightly better-feeling thought. Every time you close your eyes and see the version of life that thrills you. Every time you stop paddling and let the current hold you. Every time you let yourself not face something that isn't delightful—you're living this.

This isn't something you try to do. It's something you remember you've been doing all along.

Sometimes it's the things I barely touch that land the hardest. I don't stress about what to make for dinner—and boom, my mom comes through with lamb chops like the Universe just winked at me through a casserole dish. Or I write a two-sentence post because the words feel clean, aligned, kinda fizzy in my brain—and suddenly a whole wave of people signs up for the program I hadn't even launched yet. No pitch deck. No strategy. Just vibe.

Sometimes someone wants to have a "conversation" (you know the kind), and instead of meeting them in the emotional sandbox to build a tense little drama-castle, I just don't respond. I don't have a dog in the fight. And the moment I stop barking, the whole field clears.

That's the power of not forcing it. Not "locking it in." Just letting it land. And when I do, the Universe tends to say: "Finally. We've been holding this for you for hours." Sometimes years.

> **"What if the real spiritual breakthrough was just remembering where you put your snacks and forgiving literally everyone? Especially yourself."**

> ⇒ *Boom. Enlightenment achieved. Go drink some water.*

So don't stress about integrating this. Just let it land. Let it hum in your chest. Let it echo in your next decision. Let it guide your next sigh, your next smile, your next effortless yes.

Let it become you in the way that all truth does—softly. Quietly. Completely.

And when you forget? Beautiful. You'll remember again. And it'll be even deeper next time.

There's nowhere to get. There's only more of you to allow.

So go live. Go float. Go write your next scene.

And don't forget—Reality is optional.

☙

"What if the final step wasn't
action, but mood-based mischief?"

⟹ *Then you'd skip the strategy
meeting, follow the sparkle, and
accidentally stumble into exactly what
you wanted.*

In a robe.

The Mood Ladder (Now with 75% More Sparkles and 0% Judgment)

You don't have to leap. Just shift one notch. That's enough.

This Mood Ladder is inspired directly by the Emotional Guidance Scale shared by Abraham-Hicks—whose teachings are the vibrational foundation of this entire book. In Abraham's emotional scale there are 22 levels. This one is broken down into 7.

You can break them down into as many different levels as you like. There could be only two levels if you prefer! It's about which direction you're moving. One feels better, one feels worse.

Let it be gentle. Let it be weird. Let it be hilarious if needed. You're not climbing a corporate ladder here. You're tuning a soul-radio. One click at a time.

We'll start at the bottom—with the heaviest, hardest feelings—and move one step at a time toward relief, clarity, and joy. Each section isn't just describing the emotion—it's about how to move from one state to the next. What does it take to shift from powerlessness to a little fire? From boredom to hope? That's what this is: one gentle notch at a time, up the dial. You don't

have to rush it. Just notice what loosens, what lands, and what helps you rise.

Crushed → **Burned** You're not supposed to feel good right now. You're just supposed to feel. That ache? That weight? It means you still care. And buried under the numbness or shame or bottomed-out grief is something hot, something alive. You don't have to pretend it's okay. You just have to let the spark stir.

> Try: "What if the Universe is watching me like a sitcom and waiting for my 'finally flips the table' scene?"
>
> ⇒ *Cue applause. Character growth montage loading.*

Burned → **Fired** You felt the burn. You let yourself admit the pain. Now there's fuel in the engine. You're not lashing out, you're waking up. This isn't about revenge or punishment—it's about realizing that your emotion matters. This is anger without collapse. This is fire as forward motion.

Try: What if I stopped throwing emotional Molotovs and just wrote a strongly-worded email to my Inner Being instead?"

⇛ *Boom. Growth with flames.*

Fired → Shrunk Sometimes after the fire comes the flicker. You let it roar, and now you're left with the question: "What now?" The anger cooled, and now there's just a tired quiet—a shrinking back. That's okay. This is where you notice how far you've bent, and how ready you are to stop folding.

Try: "What if I'm not angry anymore because I'm too busy refreshing reality like it's a shipping confirmation that still says 'pending'?"

⇛ *Manifestation fatigue: it's real, it's petty, and it's here.*

Shrunk → Frayed There's nothing wrong with you for worrying. For doubting. For losing your grip a little. You're thinking a lot because you care a lot. But now it's all spiraling, and none of it feels useful. Overwhelm means your brain is overbooked. You don't need more thoughts—you need room to breathe.

Try: "What if this is just the natural consequence of pretending I could juggle flaming swords, answer emails, and become enlightened before lunch?"

⇒ Please place all expectations gently in the nearest soup.

Frayed → Flat You can stop pushing now. Let the swirl slow down. This isn't giving up—it's pressing pause. You're not chasing anything. You're not spiraling. You're just... here. Breathing. Unhooked. This is the sacred neutrality between stories. And it's not emptiness—it's rest.

Try: "What if this isn't a failure arc—it's just the mandatory bathroom break between plotlines?"

⇒ Congrats. You're now on hold with the Universe. Please enjoy this vibey elevator music.

Flat → Rising It starts small. A tiny question. A tiny lift. Maybe things could get better. Maybe I don't have to stay here. Maybe something is already shifting. You don't need certainty. You just need the willingness to look in the direction of "maybe."

Try: "What if this is the part where
the background music swells and I
remember I'm the main character
with secret powers?"

⇒ *You're not crazy. You're just early to
your own glow-up.*

Rising → **Lit** Now we're flying. The horizon opens. Your belief has turned to trust, and your trust to joy. Not because everything's fixed—but because your signal's tuned. This isn't hype. It's clarity. It's creative energy. It's alignment. And it feels like freedom.

Try: "What if this isn't optimism—
it's me mentally spending money that
hasn't arrived yet because I know the
wire transfer is pending?"

⇒ *You're not guessing. You're pre-
celebrating like a trust-fund oracle.*

Congratulations! You just climbed a ladder made of emotions, jokes, and light beams. And you didn't even break a sweat. You shifted. You tuned. You let it land.

☙

OUTRO

You Are the Dream and the Dumb Genius Who Forgot for a Minute

You don't have to hold the whole vision. Just feel for the shimmer. The glint. The glimmer. The thread that tugs.

Let your mood be the compass. Let your body be the bell. Let your life arrange itself around the signal you allow.

You are not here to effort your way to alignment. You're here to remember you already are it.

You are the dream and the dreamer. The echo and the voice. The lighthouse and the sea.

So don't just go manifest your life. Go let it meet you.

Right here. Right now. On the frequency you already knew how to tune to all along.

Maybe you'll forget. Maybe you'll spiral. Maybe you'll start narrating your resistance in Comic Sans again. Cool. Ask a better question. Laugh mid-wobble. Say, "What's the joke I'm missing that would make this whole thing funny instead of frustrating?"

Or, "What would I make if I stopped caring how it would do and started caring how it would feel?"

Let your Inner Being throw confetti every time you giggle. Let your joy be the spell. Let your mood do the manifesting.

And if all else fails? Build the cinnamon roll yacht. And let the dream dream you.

KEEP FLOATING FORWARD

This book began with one spark—one Sunday morning conversation inside the **Joy Is The Key Mastermind**. That moment carried the current forward. Insight met expression. Vibration found form. And now, here you are—holding the signal.

If you felt something unlock, you can keep the frequency alive in two effortless ways:

1. Join the Joy Is The Key Facebook Group

Come bask in the energy with over 100,000 beings who are practicing vibrational authorship in real time. It's where riffs, memes, and miracles collide daily.

[Scan to Enter the Field]

2. Enter the Mastermind That Sparked It All

Three times a week, we go live inside a sacred and hilarious container of expansion, where I share live transmissions rooted in Abraham-Hicks teachings and beyond. If this book felt like a soul frequency... the Mastermind is its living echo.

[Scan to Join the Mastermind]

Your first month is only $33 (normally $99), using code: VORTEX

☙ **Happy creating!** ❧

Made in United States
Troutdale, OR
05/31/2025

31806174R00083